Pancakes & Waffles

CHARTWELL
BOOKS, INC.

Published by Chartwell Books
a division of Book Sales, Inc.
114 Northfield Avenue
Edison, NJ 08837

This edition produced for sale
in the U.S.A., its territories
and dependencies only.
Copyright © 1995 Parragon Book Service Ltd
Copyright © 1995 in design Haldane Mason

ISBN 0-7858-04233-4

Conceived, designed and produced by Haldane Mason, London

Printed in Italy

Note: Cup measurements in this book are for standard American cups.
Unless otherwise stated, milk is assumed to be full-fat, and pepper is
freshly ground black pepper. All butter is sweet unless othwerwise
stated.

CONTENTS

TRADITIONAL PANCAKES

The traditional delicious way to eat pancakes is simply to roll them up with a squeeze of lemon and scatter of sugar. You can also serve them with fruit, or really go to town and add some cream on top!

MAKES 8

1 cup all-purpose flour

1 egg, beaten

1 egg yolk

1¼ cups milk

3 tbsp melted butter

TO SERVE

2 tbsp superfine sugar

¼ cup lemon juice

7 oz strawberries (optional)

1 Sift the flour into a bowl. Make a well in the center and add the egg, egg yolk, milk, and 2 tablespoons of the melted butter. Draw in the flour. Whisk together well and leave to rest for 30 minutes.

2 Brush a medium skillet or pancake pan with a little of the remaining butter and place over a medium heat.

3 Hold the hot pan in one hand and the pancake batter in a measuring cup in the other.

Tilt the pan and pour in about ¼ cup of the batter, tilting the pan immediately in the opposite direction so that the batter coats the base before it sets – you have to be quick.

4 When the batter has dried out on top, about 1 minute, turn the pancake over to cook on the other side – or, to impress your hungry family, toss it. To do this, hold the pan with one or both hands, tilt it away from you, shuffle the pancake toward the far edge, and flick it up into

the air, and do your best to catch it. It doesn't have to go up very high, but do not hesitate otherwise the walls and floor will be spattered! Repeat with the remaining batter.

5 Turn onto a warm serving plate, sprinkle with sugar, and squeeze over the lemon juice. Roll up and serve – with fruit, if preferred.

RATATOUILLE PANCAKES

These are a speciality of the Breton region of France, where they are always served in a square shape. The buckwheat adds a sour flavor to the pancake, and is an ideal complement to these fillings.

1 Heat the olive oil in a large pan, add the onion and garlic, and cook until soft, about 5 minutes.

2 Add the remaining ratatouille ingredients. Bring to the boil and simmer, uncovered, for 40 minutes, stirring occasionally.

3 Meanwhile, make the batter. Sift the flour and buckwheat flour into a bowl with a pinch of salt. Make a well in the center and add the eggs, apple juice, and melted butter. Draw in the flours and whisk together well. Set aside for 10 minutes.

4 Taste the ratatouille for seasoning. Cover the pan and turn off the heat.

5 Brush a skillet or pancake pan with a little oil and place over a medium high heat. Tilt the hot pan and pour in about 1½ cup of the batter, tilting the pan immediately in the opposite direction, so that the batter coats the base of the pan before it sets.

6 When the batter has dried out on top, about 3 minutes, flip the pancake over

to cook on the other side, about 1 minute. Repeat with the remaining batter to make 4 fairly thick pancakes.

7 Spoon some ratatouille mixture into the center of each pancake and fold in the 4 sides like an envelope so that a square shape is formed. Slide onto a warmed serving plate and serve piping hot.

BRETON BUCKWHEAT PANCAKES

If you ever pay a visit to Brittany, France, don't leave without sampling the deliciously sweet local mussels. In this recipe, they are served in buckwheat pancakes.

SERVES 4–6

2 lb mussels in their shells

4 whole garlic cloves

2 tbsp butter

2 shallots, chopped finely

13 oz chopped tomatoes

1 tsp saffron threads, crushed

3 tbsp white wine

1 tbsp light cream

2 tbsp chopped fresh parsley

BATTER

½ cup all-purpose flour

½ cup buckwheat flour

2 eggs, beaten

1¼ cups dry sparkling white wine

¼ cup melted butter

salt

oil for brushing

1 Clean the mussels, removing the beards. Discard any mussels that are open.

2 To make the batter, sift the flours into a bowl, make a well in the center and add the eggs, a pinch of salt, the sparkling wine, and melted butter. Whisk together well and set aside for 10 minutes.

3 To make the sauce, put the mussels into a large pan with ⅔ cup water and 3 of the garlic cloves. Cover and simmer for 7–8 minutes. Remove from the heat and drain, reserving the cooking liquor. Set the mussels aside, discarding any that are still closed. Shell the mussels, reserving 8–12 in their shells for garnish.

4 Return the cooking liquor to the pan with the butter, shallots, and the remaining garlic clove, crushed, and cook until the shallots have softened, about 3 minutes. Stir in the tomatoes, saffron, white wine, and cream. Cook for 8–10 minutes until the liquor is reduced. Stir the mussels into the sauce. Keep warm over a low heat.

8

5 Brush a skillet or pancake pan with a little oil and place over a medium high heat. Tilt the hot pan and pour in about ½ cup of the batter, tilting the pan immediately in the opposite direction, so that the batter coats the base before it sets.

6 When the batter has dried out on top, about 3 minutes, turn the pancake over to cook on the other side, 2 minutes. Slide onto a warmed serving plate. Repeat with the remaining batter. Makes 4–6.

7 Spoon some sauce into the center of each pancake. Fold up the 4 edges like a loose envelope. Garnish with the reserved mussels, sprinkle with chopped parsley, and serve.

POTATO PANCAKES WITH SAUSAGES

This is a hearty, tasty dish for a winter's day. It is best to use sausages that are strongly flavored with garlic, available from many delicatessens.

SERVES 4

½ cup all-purpose flour

1 egg, beaten

1 tsp oil

1¼ cups milk

2 cups grated white potatoes

olive oil for brushing

FILLING

1 tbsp olive oil

1 lb sausages, cut into 1 inch pieces

1 celery stalk, sliced

4 cups shredded Savoy cabbage,

salt and pepper

1 Sift the flour and a pinch of salt into a bowl. Make a well in the center and add the egg, oil, and milk. Whisk together well. Set aside for 30 minutes, then stir the grated potato into the batter. Use immediately.

2 Brush a skillet or pancake pan with a little olive oil and place over a medium high heat. Make 2 small pancakes at a time, using about ¼ cup batter for each one. Alternatively, make 1 large pancake, using ½ cup batter. Cook both large and small pancakes for 3–4 minutes on each side, and stack on a baking tray to keep warm, covered.

3 Heat 1 tablespoon olive oil in a skillet, add the sausages, and cook quickly, stirring constantly, until they are sealed on all sides. Add the sliced celery and the shredded cabbage, reduce the heat to medium, and cook for 5 minutes. Season well.

4 Put 3 small potato pancakes or 1 large pancake per person onto each warmed serving plate and spoon over the

10

sausage mixture. Serve piping
hot.

GRAVADLAX PANCAKES

Gravadlax is marinated salmon, and it is used here to make a sophisticated supper or brunch dish. The dill flavor in the marinade should be quite strong.

SERVES 4

1 tsp sugar

4 tbsp chopped fresh dill

2 tbsp sunflower oil

1 tbsp lemon juice

1 tbsp green peppercorn mustard

10 oz smoked salmon

salt and pepper

thinly sliced cucumber

fresh dill sprigs, to garnish

BATTER

1 cup wholewheat flour

pinch of salt

2 eggs, beaten

1¼ cups milk

1 tbsp melted butter

1 tsp green peppercorn mustard

oil for brushing

1 Combine the sugar, dill, oil, lemon juice, and mustard in a non-porous, non-metallic dish. Slice the smoked salmon and lay it in this marinade. Sprinkle over the salt and pepper. Leave to marinate for 1½ hours in the refrigerator. Remove and let it come to room temperature.

2 To make the batter, sift the flour into a bowl to aerate it and make a well in the center. Add the remaining ingredients and whisk together well.

3 Brush a skillet or pancake pan with oil and place over a medium high heat. Spoon 3 tbsp of batter into the hot pan, to make one 4 inch pancake. When the top of the pancake has dried out, about 2–3 minutes, turn it over to cook on the other side for a minute or so. Make 8 pancakes. Stack the pancakes on a baking tray, cover, and keep warm.

4 Put 2 pancakes onto a warmed serving plate. Spoon a quarter of the sliced cucumber on and put a quarter of the gravadlax salmon on top. Repeat with the remaining pancakes, salmon, and cucumber. Garnish with dill sprigs.

WALNUT & BLUE CHEESE PANCAKES

Look out for fresh walnuts in the fall. They are sweet, moist, and have none of the harsh dryness that shelled walnuts do. However, you will need a good pair of nutcrackers!

SERVES 4

½ cup all-purpose flour

½ cup wholewheat flour

3 tbsp ground walnuts, toasted lightly

1 egg, beaten

1 egg yolk

1¼ cups milk

1 tbsp oil

salt

1 tbsp walnut oil for brushing

FILLING

6 oz blue cheese, roughly chopped

1 celery stalk, blanched and chopped

3 tbsp chopped walnuts

1 Combine the flours, ground walnuts, and a pinch of salt in a bowl. Make a well in the center and add the egg, egg yolk, milk, and oil. Set aside for 30 minutes.

2 Brush a skillet or pancake pan with some of the walnut oil and place over a medium high heat. Tilt the pan and pour in about ¼ cup of the batter, tilting the pan immediately in the opposite direction so that the batter coats the base before it sets. Cook for 1 minute until the batter has dried out on top. Turn the pancake over and sprinkle with a little of the blue cheese and chopped celery. Let the cheese melt while the second side of the pancake cooks for 1 minute.

3 Repeat with the remaining batter, cheese, and celery. Makes 8 pancakes.

4 Sprinkle some chopped walnuts over each pancake and then roll up. Serve piping hot.

PANCAKES WITH CRABMEAT FILLING

Very good quality crabmeat is available frozen out of the shell, which saves all the bother of preparing the whole crab. It is sold in mixed packs, half brown, half white meat.

SERVES 4–6

½ cup all-purpose flour

½ cup wholewheat flour

1 tsp baking powder

2 eggs, beaten

scant 1 cup milk

2 tbsp oil

FILLING

4 tbsp fresh white breadcrumbs

4 oz white crabmeat

4 oz brown crabmeat

2 hard-cooked eggs, chopped

2 tbsp mayonnaise

salt and pepper

2 tbsp chopped fresh parsley

1 tsp mustard powder

½ tsp chili powder

1 Sift the flours and baking powder into a bowl. Make a well in the center and add the eggs, milk, 1 tablespoon of the oil, and seasoning. Whisk together well and leave to rest for 10 minutes.

2 Mix together the breadcrumbs, both crabmeats, the eggs, and mayonnaise. Season well.

3 Combine the parsley, mustard powder, and chili powder in a small bowl. Set aside.

4 Brush a skillet or pancake pan with a little of the remaining oil and place over a medium heat. Spoon in 2–3 tablespoons of the batter at a time, to make 3 inch diameter pancakes. When the batter has dried out on top, after about 1 minute, turn over and cook for 1 minute. Keep warm in the oven while you make the remaining 11 pancakes.

5 Put 2 or 3 pancakes on each warm serving plate, depending on how hungry everyone is, and spoon on the

dressed crabmeat. Sprinkle over
a little of the parsley mixture
and serve with a green salad.

SPRING ASPARAGUS PANCAKES

It is possible nowadays to eat strawberries and asparagus in midwinter and chestnuts in midsummer. But do they taste good? Seasonal produce is both cheaper and tastier in its original season, and summer is the season when asparagus comes into its own.

SERVES 4

1 quantity Traditional Pancake Batter (see page 4)

24 asparagus stalks, peeled

HOLLANDAISE SAUCE

2 egg yolks

1 tsp malt vinegar

1 bayleaf

1 cup butter, melted and cooled

salt and pepper

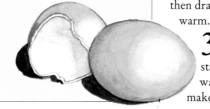

1 Add a pinch of salt to the batter and use to make 8 small thick pancakes, about 5 inches in diameter. Cover and keep warm.

2 Put the asparagus into a large pan of boiling lightly salted water. Blanch for 2–3 minutes, then drain thoroughly. Keep warm.

3 Wrap each pancake around 3 asparagus stalks and set aside on warm plates while you make the Hollandaise sauce.

4 Set a heatproof bowl over a pan of barely simmering water. Put the egg yolks and vinegar into the bowl and whisk until pale. Add the bayleaf. Add the melted butter gradually, whisking all the time until the sauce is thick. Season with pepper. Remove the bayleaf.

5 Put 2 asparagus pancakes on each of 4 warmed serving plates. Spoon over the Hollandaise, and serve warm.

RICOTTA & SPINACH CRESPOLINI

Pancakes are made in different forms around the world and from different flours; this is what the Italians do to them.

1 quantity Traditional Pancake Batter (see page 4)

1½ cups frozen or fresh spinach, chopped

3 cups Ricotta or farmers' cheese

pinch of grated nutmeg

4 tbsp grated Parmesan cheese

1 tbsp chopped fresh flat-leafed parsley

4 sun-dried tomatoes, chopped

1 cup all-purpose flour

2 eggs, beaten lightly

1 tbsp butter

salt and pepper

1 Grease a round or square casserole, large enough to hold a pancake flat. Add a pinch of salt to the batter and make 6 pancakes (see page 4). Set aside.

2 If using fresh spinach, first put the spinach into a dry pan and set over a medium heat. Stir constantly for 2 minutes. Remove from the heat.

3 Combine the spinach, Ricotta or farmers' cheese, nutmeg, 2 tablespoons of the Parmesan cheese, parsley, and tomatoes in a large bowl. Season well. Stir in the flour and eggs.

4 Lay a pancake in the bottom of the casserole and spoon over a fifth of the spinach filling. Layer pancakes and filling alternately, ending with a pancake. Spoon over any leftover filling and sprinkle over the remaining Parmesan cheese. Cover with a lid or foil.

5 Place in a preheated oven at 350°F for 40 minutes.

6 Cut into 6 wedges and serve immediately, piping hot.

PANCAKES STUFFED WITH CHICKEN & TARRAGON BUTTER

SERVES 4

1 quantity Traditional Pancake Batter (see page 4)

¼ cup butter

12 oz chicken breasts, cut into strips 2 x ½ x ½ inches

2 leeks, sliced

4 tbsp chopped fresh tarragon

corn salad to serve (optional)

salt and pepper

tarragon, to garnish

lemon slices, to garnish

This is a very simple, classic recipe where the taste of the tarragon is really pronounced.

1 Add a pinch of salt to the batter and use to make 8 pancakes (see page 4). Set aside to keep warm.

2 Melt the butter in a skillet and add the chicken and leek. Cook over a medium heat for 5 minutes, stirring frequently. Add the tarragon and season well.

3 Lay 1 pancake flat. Spoon the chicken mixture down the center of the pancake and roll it up. Repeat with the remaining pancakes.

4 Put the rolled up pancakes onto warmed serving plates and spoon over a little tarragon butter from the pan. Serve with corn salad, or garnish with tarragon and lemon slices, if you prefer.

STIR-FRIED BEEF IN CORIANDER (CILANTRO) ROLL

SERVES 4

2 tbsp chopped fresh cilantro

pinch of salt

1 quantity Traditional Pancake Batter (see page 4)

2 tbsp sunflower oil

1 tsp sesame oil

2 scallions, sliced finely

½ green bell pepper, sliced

8 oz sirloin steak, sliced thinly across the grain

1 inch ginger, grated

1 garlic clove, crushed

2 tbsp black bean sauce

fresh cilantro sprigs, to garnish

These quickly cooked pancakes with stir-fried beef can be rustled up in a hurry. Make sure the pancakes are nicely thin and crisp and not at all soggy.

1 Stir the cilantro and a pinch of salt into the pancake batter.

2 Brush a skillet or pancake pan with a little of the sunflower oil and place over a medium heat. Tilt the pan and pour in 2 tablespoons of the batter, immediately tilting the pan so that the batter coats the base before it sets. Cook for about 2 minutes on each side. Repeat with the remaining batter, stirring it before making each pancake. Make 8 pancakes. Keep the pancakes warm in a low oven, while you make the filling.

3 Heat the sesame oil and remaining sunflower oil in a wok or large skillet. Add the scallions, bell peppers, and beef. Stir-fry for 2 minutes and then add the ginger root and garlic.

4 Stir in the black bean sauce and cook for 1 minute more. Remove from the heat.

5 Lay a pancake flat. Spoon some filling onto one half of the pancake and fold over the other half. Repeat with the remaining pancakes. Put two pancakes on each warmed serving plate, garnish with cilantro sprigs and serve immediately piping hot.

TRADITIONAL WAFFLES

Waffles are particularly delicious cooked fresh for breakfast and served with crisp bacon instead of ice cream.

MAKES 8–10

2 cups self-rising flour

2 tbsp superfine sugar

3 eggs, separated

generous 1½ cups milk

⅓ cup butter, melted

1 tsp vanilla extract

melted butter for brushing

¾ cup maple syrup

2 cups vanilla ice cream

1 Sift the flour and sugar into a bowl. Add the egg yolks, milk, melted butter, and vanilla. Whisk together well. Beat the egg whites until stiff. Fold into the waffle batter until thoroughly combined.

2 Heat a waffle iron to medium high and brush with a little melted butter. Pour on sufficient batter to cover two-thirds of the waffle iron. Close the 2 halves and cook for about 1 minute, turning over halfway to cook for 1 minute on each side if the waffle iron is a manual one.

3 Turn out onto a warm serving plate. Pour over a little maple syrup and spoon on some vanilla ice cream.

4 The waffles can be made up to 24 hours in advance and reheated in the toaster or under the broiler before serving.

26

POTATO WAFFLES WITH GOAT'S CHEESE

SERVES 4

2 eggs, beaten lightly

3 tbsp all-purpose flour

2 tbsp olive oil

1 large onion, grated

2 large potatoes, grated

1 cup arugula leaves

2 tbsp extra virgin olive oil

1 tsp green peppercorns in brine

6 oz firm goat's cheese, crumbled, or sharp Cheddar, shaved

3 slices bacon, cooked until crisp, chopped finely (optional)

salt and pepper

Waffles are usually made from a richer batter than that used for pancakes . They can also be very decorative, especially if you use a waffle iron, which has either a rectangular or a square latticed design, or an attractive heart-shaped design.

1 Whisk together the eggs, flour, and 1 tablespoon of the olive oil. Add the grated onion and potato.

2 Heat your waffle iron to medium heat and brush with some of the remaining olive oil. Pour in enough batter to cover two-thirds of the hot waffle iron, close the 2 halves together and cook for about 7 minutes, until brown, turning over half way if the waffle iron is a manual one to cook for 7 minutes on each side. Put on a wire rack to keep warm in a low oven while you make the remaining waffles.

3 Toss the arugula leaves in the extra virgin olive oil, seasoning, and green peppercorns. Divide between the waffles.

4 Divide the goat's cheese, and bacon if using, between the waffles and serve.

POTATO WAFFLES WITH SMOKED TROUT

SERVES 4

2 eggs, beaten lightly

3 tbsp all-purpose flour

2 tbsp olive oil

1 large onion, grated

2 large potatoes, grated

5 tbsp mayonnaise

2 tbsp water

1 tbsp wholegrain mustard

8 oz smoked trout fillets, flaked

4 scallions, sliced finely

½ cucumber, peeled and diced

8 sweet dill pickles, sliced

salt and pepper

green salad, to serve

After the potatoes have been grated use them instantly or they will go black. For a crisper finish, waffles can be finished in the oven on a wire rack.

1 Whisk together the eggs, flour, and 1 tablespoon of the olive oil. Add the onion and potato.

2 Heat your waffle iron to medium heat and brush with the remaining olive oil. Pour in the batter to cover two-thirds of the area. Close the 2 halves together and cook for about 7 minutes, turning over to cook for 7 minutes on each side if the waffle iron is a manual one.

3 Transfer to a preheated oven at 325°F on a wire rack while you make the remaining waffles.

4 Meanwhile, mix the mayonnaise, water, and mustard together in a bowl. Add the flaked trout and combine thoroughly.

5 Put the waffles onto warmed serving plates and divide the trout mayonnaise between them. Sprinkle over the scallions, cucumber, and sweet dill pickles. Season well and serve with a green salad.

Potato Waffles with Smoked Trout

CHIVE WAFFLES WITH CREAM CHEESE

Potato waffles are a good carrier for lots of different herbs and spices – try a pinch of paprika in the mixture, or chopped parsley.

SERVES 4-6

2 eggs, beaten lightly

3 tbsp all-purpose flour

2 tbsp olive oil

4 tbsp chopped fresh chives

1 large onion, grated

1 lb white potatoes

salt and pepper

TOPPING

2 tbsp butter

2 leeks, sliced

½ cup full-fat cream cheese

1 egg, beaten

1 tbsp chopped fresh thyme

1 tbsp chopped fresh oregano

salt and pepper

1 Combine the eggs, flour, 1 tablespoon of the olive oil, pepper, and chives in a bowl. Stir in the onion and grate the potatoes straight into the bowl.

2 Brush the waffle iron with the remaining olive oil. Heat it to a medium heat and spoon in 4 tablespoons of the waffle batter. Close the 2 halves and cook for 7 minutes, turning over to cook for 7 minutes on each side if the waffle iron is a manual one. Transfer to a wire rack and keep warm in the oven while you make the remaining waffles.

3 Melt the butter in a skillet and soften the leeks, about 5 minutes.

4 Mix the cream cheese, egg, thyme, oregano, and seasoning together.

5 Put the waffles onto a broiler rack, spoon on the leeks and the cream cheese mixture, dividing them equally between the waffles, and cook under a preheated broiler for 4–5 minutes. Serve piping hot.

HORSERADISH BLINIS WITH DILL CREAM

MAKES 80

2 tsp dried yeast

1 cup warm milk

1 cup wholewheat flour

salt and pepper

1 cup all-purpose flour

2 eggs, beaten

3 tbsp melted butter

¼ cup water

1 egg white

oil for brushing

fresh dill sprigs to garnish

DILL CREAM

1 tbsp horseradish relish

2 cups sour cream

1 tsp grated lemon rind

2 cups chopped dill

There are many pancake recipes from around the world, but blinis are unique among them as they are leavened with yeast to give a rich, moist batter. Originating in Russia, they make excellent finger food for parties.

1 Sprinkle the yeast onto the warm milk and set aside for about 15 minutes.

2 Sift the wholewheat flour and a pinch of salt into a large bowl, make a well in the center and add the yeast mixture. Cover with plastic wrap and leave in a warm place until doubled in size, about 20–30 minutes.

3 Sift the all-purpose flour into a bowl. Make a well in the center and add the eggs, melted butter, and water.

Draw in the flour and beat until smooth. Stir into the wholewheat flour mixture.

4 Cover the bowl with plastic wrap, and leave it to rise in the refrigerator overnight.

5 Combine the horseradish relish, sour cream, lemon rind, and dill together in a bowl. Season, then cover, and chill in the refrigerator.

6 Whisk the egg white until stiff and fold into the blini batter until well combined.

7 Heat a little oil in a skillet or pancake pan. Drop in teaspoonfuls of the batter, 4 at a time, evenly spaced around the pan. Cook over a medium heat for 1–2 minutes and when bubbles rise to the surface, turn over and cook for no more than 1 minute. Transfer to a baking tray, cover, and keep warm in a low oven.

8 When the batter is all used, arrange the blinis on a warm serving dish and put small amounts of the dill cream on each one, about ½ teaspoon per blini. Garnish and serve.

35

LOBSTER BLINIS

Blinis are usually served as a sophisticated accompaniment to luxury foods, such as caviar and other roes. Here I have paired larger blinis with a lobster mixture for a delicate lunch dish. Crabmeat can be bought in cans or frozen.

SERVES 4

1 quantity Blini mix (see page 34)

1 egg white

TOPPING

1 tbsp butter

1 tbsp all-purpose flour

2 tbsp light cream

½ cup milk

¼ tsp chili powder

1 tbsp brandy

⅓ cup white crabmeat

½ cup lobster meat (if not available use crabmeat)

pepper

TO SERVE

½ iceberg lettuce, shredded

½ cucumber, sliced thinly

2 tomatoes, sliced thinly

4 tbsp chopped fresh parsley

5 lemon slices, halved, to garnish

1 Make the blini mix as on page 34, cover and leave overnight in the refrigerator.

2 Next day, melt the butter in a pan. Remove from the heat and stir in the flour. Whisk in the cream and milk. Return to the heat and bring to the boil, stirring constantly.

3 Stir in the chili powder and brandy. Add the crabmeat and lobster meat. Remove from the heat. Sprinkle with pepper, cover, and keep warm.

4 Whisk the egg white until stiff and fold into the blini batter until thoroughly combined.

5 Heat a little oil in a skillet or pancake pan. Drop in 2 tablespoons of the batter at a time to make 4 inch diameter blinis. When bubbles rise to the surface, after 2–3 minutes, turn over and cook for about 1–2 minutes. Keep warm on a baking tray while you make the remaining blinis.

6 Put 2 blinis, overlapping each other, on each warmed serving plate. Arrange a quarter

36

of the lettuce, cucumber, and tomato together on the side of each plate. Spoon over a quarter of the lobster topping on top.

Sprinkle on some chopped parsley and garnish with a lemon slice. Serve while still warm.

SALMON ROE CANAPES

This is the classic way to serve blinis. Salmon roe, which is pink, and lumpfish caviar, which is black, are sold in tiny jars in many supermarkets. The caviars look stunning together perched on the sour cream.

MAKES 80

2 tsp dried yeast

⅔ cup warm milk

1 cup wholewheat flour

1 cup all-purpose flour

2 eggs, beaten

3 tbsp melted butter

¼ cup warm milk

¼ cup water

1 egg white

oil for brushing

1¼ cups sour cream

2 oz salmon roe

1 oz lumpfish caviar

salt and pepper

3 lemons, sliced thinly and quartered, to garnish

1 Make the blini batter as on page 34 and leave overnight in the refrigerator.

2 Next day, beat the egg white until stiff peaks form and fold into the mix until thoroughly combined.

3 Brush a skillet or pancake pan with a little oil and heat through. Over a medium-high heat drop in teaspoonfuls of the batter, evenly spaced in the pan. When bubbles rise to the surface, after 1–2 minutes, turn the blinis over and cook briefly on the second side. Keep warm on a covered baking tray while you make the rest.

4 When all the batter has been used, arrange the warmish blinis on a serving dish and put onto each one about ½ teaspoon of sour cream and a little salmon roe and lumpfish caviar – I find it easiest to pop this on from the end of a teaspoon.

38

5 Garnish each canapé with a lemon quarter and a sprinkling of pepper.

39

CORNMEAL PONES WITH DOWNHOME BEANS

This recipe combines an unleavened cornmeal bread with a delicious bean dish, to make a simple, filling, and tasty version of a staple cowboy meal. Use a quick-cook kind of cornmeal.

SERVES 4–6

2 tbsp vegetable oil

1 red onion, chopped

1 green bell pepper, chopped

4 slices bacon

2 tsp ground cilantro

7 oz chopped tomatoes

1 tbsp tomato paste

½ tsp chili flakes

14 oz can cannellini beans

14 oz can borlotti beans

PONES

1½ cups cornmeal

1½ cups water

2 eggs, beaten

1 cup milk

½ cup all-purpose flour

3 tbsp butter, melted

salt and pepper

1 Heat 1 tablespoon of the vegetable oil in a large pan and add the onion, garlic, and green bell pepper. Cook for 2 minutes. Chop each bacon slice into 4 pieces and add to the pan. Stir in the cilantro, chopped tomatoes, and tomato paste. Bring to a gentle boil and simmer for 10 minutes.

2 Stir in the chili flakes. Drain the two types of beans and stir into the mix. Taste for seasoning. Cover and keep warm over a low heat.

3 Boil the water and put into a bowl. Stir in the cornmeal and salt. Leave to stand for 10 minutes, then add the eggs, beating well. Beat in the flour and butter.

4 Brush a skillet or pancake pan with some of the remaining oil and drop in about ¼ cup of the cornmeal batter. Make sure it does not spread too far. Cook for 2–3 minutes on each side. Keep warm while you make the remaining pones.

5 Put 3 pones on each warmed serving plate and spoon over the beans. Serve piping hot.

NEW ENGLAND FLAPJACK BREAKFAST

Maple syrup – from the sap of the maple tree – and honey are the most natural sweeteners that you can buy. It takes 8 buckets of sap to make 1 bucket of syrup, which explains its high price.

SERVES 4

1 cup all-purpose flour

1 tsp baking powder

1 egg, beaten

1 egg yolk

scant 1 cup milk

2 tbsp melted butter

pinch of salt

FILLING

12 slices maple smoked bacon

8 small sausages (optional)

8 eggs

2 tbsp butter

½ cup maple syrup

salt and pepper

1 Sift the flour and baking powder into a bowl. Make a well in the center and add the egg, egg yolk, milk, 1 tablespoon of the melted butter, and a pinch of salt. Whisk together well.

2 Put the bacon and sausages, if using, on a wire rack set over a baking tray. Place in a preheated oven at 350°F for 10–12 minutes.

3 Meanwhile, put the eggs and seasoning into a bowl and beat well. Put the butter into a large pan.

4 Brush a skillet or pancake pan with the remaining melted butter and spoon in 2 tablespoons of the batter. Do not let it spread to more than 4 inches. Cook 3 pancakes at a time, until the batter is used. Stack on a baking tray and cover to keep warm.

5 To make the scrambled eggs, put the large pan over a

gentle heat to melt the butter. Add the eggs and stir constantly for 2 minutes; they will continue cooking while you serve them.

6 Serve 2 sausages, if using, 3 slices of bacon and a spoonful of scrambled eggs on each plate. Stack 3 pancakes up and transfer to the plate. Serve the maple syrup separately.

CREPES AU CHOCOLAT

If there are chocoholics among you, you may want to add more melted chocolate to this recipe – but this is enough for me!

SERVES 4–8

1 quantity Traditional Pancake Batter (see page 4)

3½ squares dark chocolate, melted

1 tbsp superfine sugar

2 tbsp melted butter

3 cups fresh or frozen raspberries

CUSTARD

2½ cups milk

⅓ cup superfine sugar

1 tbsp all-purpose flour

6 egg yolks

1 Combine the pancake batter with the melted chocolate and 1 tablespoon superfine sugar.

2 Brush a skillet or pancake pan with a little of the melted butter. Holding the pan over a medium heat, tilt it to one side. Add about ¼ cup of the chocolate pancake batter and immediately tilt the pan in the other direction, so that the batter coats the base. Turn the pancake after about 1 minute, to cook the other side briefly, less than a minute. Do not let it burn or cook over too high a heat. Stack on a covered baking tray to keep warm. Make 8 pancakes.

3 Bring the milk to boiling point, until the surface shivers. Remove from the heat.

4 Whisk together the sugar, flour, and egg yolks in a bowl until pale. Add the scalded milk slowly, whisking all the time.

5 Transfer to a pan over a low heat, stirring constantly until the mixture thickens. Do not boil. Strain.

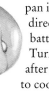

6 To serve, spoon custard onto a plate, fold 2 pancakes into quarters and tuck some raspberries into each one. Serve warm.

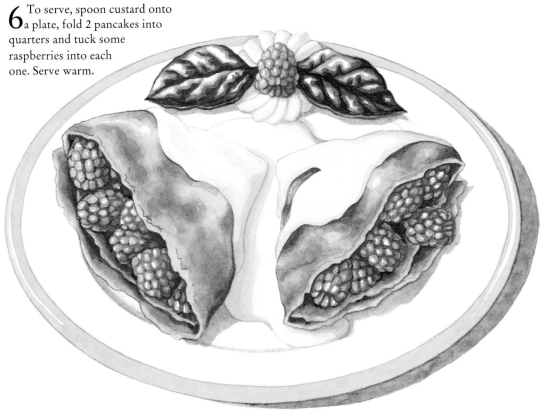

CREPES SUZETTE

The classic French dessert! If you do flambé the crêpes, spread the flaming liqueur over the whole plate and blow out the flames, before the plate gets too hot but also before all of the alcohol burns off!

SERVES 4–6

1 quantity Traditional Pancake Batter (see page 4)

grated rind of 1 orange

1 cup granulated sugar

⅔ cup water

rind of 1 orange, white pith shaved off, cut into thin strips

2 tbsp butter, melted

juice of 1 orange

1 cup orange liqueur, such as Cointreau

1 Combine the pancake batter with the grated orange rind. Set aside.

2 Put the sugar and water into a medium pan and bring to a gentle boil. Add the strips of orange rind and cook gently until the syrup coats the back of a spoon, about 5 minutes. Set aside.

3 Meanwhile, brush a skillet or pancake pan with a little of the melted butter and place over a medium heat. Tilt the pan and pour in about ¼ cup of the batter, tilting the pan immediately in the opposite direction, so that the batter coats the base. After about 1 minute, or when the batter has dried on top, turn the pancake over and cook on the other side for another minute. Make 8–12 pancakes.

4 Put 2 pancakes flat on each warmed large plate.

5 Reheat the syrup and stir in the orange juice and ⅔ cup of the liqueur. Pour a little over each plate.

46

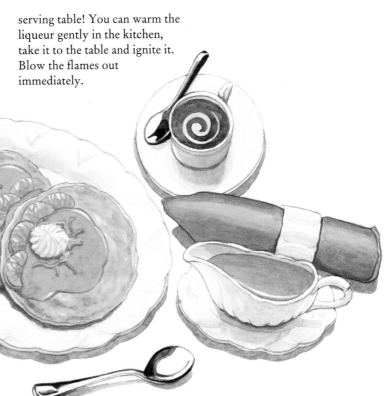

6 Heat the remaining liqueur gently in a small lipped pan. It may ignite itself, but if not, set a match to it and pour over the pancakes immediately. This is most effective if done at the serving table! You can warm the liqueur gently in the kitchen, take it to the table and ignite it. Blow the flames out immediately.

SUMMER FRUIT LAYER

1 quantity Traditional Pancake Batter (see page 4)

2 cups strawberries, fresh or frozen, halved

2 cups raspberries, fresh or frozen

2½ cups blueberries, fresh or frozen

1½ cups blackcurrants, fresh or frozen

rind of ½ lemon in one large piece

4 tbsp confectioner's sugar

½ cup whipped cream

This is based on a traditional Finnish recipe, their version of Summer Pudding. The berries can be enjoyed cooked whole with no elaboration, apart from my addition of cream. Put the layers together at the last minute and the flavours will stay distinct.

1 Make 5 pancakes from the pancake batter, as described on page 4.

2 Put half of the fruit into a pan with the lemon rind and confectioner's sugar, bring to the boil and simmer for 15–20 minutes, until thick and syrupy. Reserve some uncooked fruit for the garnish.

3 Choose a dish with a small lip around the edge to hold the juice from the fruit and put the first pancake on the bottom.

Spoon over the remaining blueberries and 5 tablespoons of the stewed fruit, followed by the second pancake. Spoon over the remaining blackcurrants and 4 tablespoons of the stewed fruit. Put the third pancake on top, spoon over the remaining raspberries and 4 tablespoons of the stewed fruit. Cover with another pancake and the remaining strawberries.

48

Spoon over 4 tablespoons of the
stewed fruit and lay the last
pancake on top. Pour over any
remaining stewed fruit, and
garnish with the reserved
uncooked fruit.

4 Cut into wedges, and
serve immediately with
a little whipped cream.

ORANGE SOUFFLE PANCAKES

Traditional pancakes are filled with a light, delicately flavoured orange filling for an elegant dessert.

SERVES 4
1 quantity Traditional Pancake Batter (see page 4)
grated rind of 2 oranges
6 tbsp ground hazelnuts, toasted
1 cup milk
2 egg yolks
¼ cup superfine sugar
3 tbsp all-purpose flour
4 egg whites

1 Combine the pancake batter with the grated rind of 1 orange. Make 8 large pancakes from the batter, using 2 tablespoonsful for each one, cooking for 1 minute on each side. The pancakes should be fairly thin and delicate.

2 When each pancake has finished cooking, before turning it out of the pan, sprinkle 1 tablespoon of the hazelnuts over it, fold in half and then in half again. Transfer to a baking tray.

3 Bring the milk nearly to boiling point, until the surface shivers. Beat together the egg yolks, half of the sugar, the remaining grated orange rind, and the flour, until thick. Whisk in the hot milk and return to the milk pan. Bring to the boil and simmer for 2 minutes, whisking constantly. Remove from the heat.

4 Whisk the egg whites until stiff, add the remaining sugar and continue whisking until stiff. Spoon a

quarter of the egg white into the mixture in the pan. Stir well to combine. Add the remaining egg white and fold in lightly until thoroughly combined.

5 Spoon 4 tablespoons of the mixture

underneath the top layer only of each pancake. Place in a preheated oven at 400°F for 15 minutes. Serve immediately.

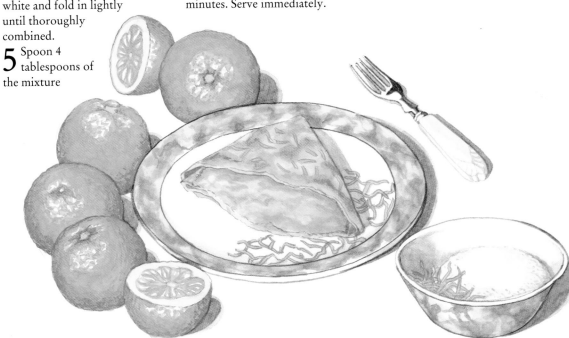

APRICOT PANCAKES

½ cup all-purpose flour

½ cup wholewheat flour

1 egg, beaten

1 egg yolk

1¼ cups milk

1 tbsp oil

1 lb fresh apricots, halved, pits removed

⅓ cup superfine sugar

2 tbsp water

1 tsp ground cinnamon

pinch of ground mace

1 tbsp natural yogurt

oil for brushing

There are times when most of us have to pull our belts in and watch what we eat. This recipe is for those times – healthy but deliciously satisfying.

1 Sift the flours into a bowl. Make a well in the center and add the egg, egg yolk, milk, and oil. Whisk well to combine. Leave to rest for 20–30 minutes.

2 Meanwhile, put the apricots, sugar, water, cinnamon, and mace into a pan and bring to a gentle boil. Simmer for 10 minutes. Remove half of the apricot halves and set aside. Cook the remaining apricots for a further 10 minutes. Strain into a pitcher and stir in the yogurt. Keep the apricots warm while you make the pancakes.

3 Brush a skillet or pancake pan with a little oil and place over a medium heat. Tilt the pan and pour in about ⅓ cup of the batter, tilting the pan immediately in the opposite direction so that the batter coats the base. When the batter has dried on top, after 3–4 minutes, turn the pancake over and cook the other side for about 1 minute. Repeat with the remaining batter to make 6 pancakes.

4 When the pancakes are cooked, slide onto warmed serving plates and spoon a few

whole apricots down the middle
of each one. Roll up the
pancakes and pour over a little
of the apricot sauce.

FLAMBEED BANANA WAFFLES

This is a stunner! Serve it after a barbecue or to end a weekend lunch. The combination of bananas, rum, and amaretto cookies is wonderful.

SERVES 6

1 quantity Traditional Waffle mix (see page 26)

½ cup butter

6 bananas, peeled and halved lengthwise

1 cup superfine sugar

¼ cup water

¾ cup dark rum

3 cups crumbled amaretto cookies

ice cream, to serve

1 Make 12 waffles (see page 26). Keep warm.

2 Melt the butter in a large skillet and put in the bananas. Increase the heat and cook them for 1 minute, then turn and cook for 1 minute on the other side.

3 Put 2 waffles on each warmed serving plate and lay 1 banana half across each waffle.

4 Add the sugar and water to the pan juices and bring to the boil. Simmer for about 5 minutes until syrupy. Divide the sauce among the 6 plates.

5 Put the rum into a small lipped pan and heat gently. It may ignite by itself, but if it does not, very carefully, light it with a match and pour a little immediately over each plate. You may be happier to do this in smaller amounts.

Blow out the flames before all the alcohol burns off. Sprinkle over the amaretto cookies and serve with ice cream.

55

CARAMELIZED VANILLA WAFFLES

SERVES 6

½ quantity Traditional Waffle
Batter (see page 26)

2 cups vanilla ice cream

1 cup granulated sugar

½ cup water

This is a thrill to make because it produces a wonderful effect, yet is very simple. Handle the hot sugar with care, because it reaches an extremely high temperature.

1 Make 6 waffles following the recipe. Place 1 on each serving plate.

2 Scoop ice cream onto each waffle and put into the freezer or refrigerator while making the sauce.

3 Put the sugar and water into a pan and heat gently, stirring, until the sugar has dissolved. Bring to the boil and boil for about 10 minutes, until the sugar turns dark golden brown. Make sure that you do not get any foreign bodies into the sugar as this will make it crystallize, in which case you will have to start again. As an extra precaution, I always brush the side of the pan down with water; this removes any sugar that may stick to it and crystallize, causing the rest of the sugar to do the same.

4 When all of the sugar is this rich dark golden brown color, remove the waffles from the freezer or refrigerator and pour a little of the caramelized sugar over each one. It will harden instantly on the ice cream and waffle. Serve immediately.

56

HAZELNUT PRALINE WAFFLES

Do not be put off by the amount of sugar in this recipe; it is the smallest amount to use that is practical to make a praline and a caramel sauce.

SERVES 6

1 quantity Traditional Waffle Batter (see page 26)

6 tbsp ground hazelnuts, toasted

2 tbsp butter, melted

2 cups granulated sugar

¾ cup water

4 tbsp chopped hazelnuts

½ cup light cream

2 cups vanilla ice cream

1 Combine the waffle batter and ground hazelnuts. Heat your waffle iron to medium high and brush with melted butter. Pour on enough batter to cover two-thirds of the iron and close the 2 halves. Cook for 2 minutes, turning over half way to cook for 1 minute on each side if the waffle iron is a manual one. Turn out onto a wire rack, and make 5 more waffles.

2 Put 1 cup of the sugar into a pan with ⅓ cup of the water. Bring to the boil and simmer gently until it starts to

change color to golden brown. In order to catch it at the right stage, when the color reaches a dark brown, drop a little onto a plate; if it turns rock hard, it is ready. Stir in the chopped hazelnuts and pour onto a metal baking tray. It should harden quite quickly.

3 Put the remaining sugar and water into a pan and bring to the boil. Simmer gently until the sugar changes color. Have ready a large bowl of iced water. When the syrup reaches a golden color, about 20 minutes, remove from the heat and put the base of the pan into the cold water to

prevent any further cooking. Stir
in the cream and leave
to set.

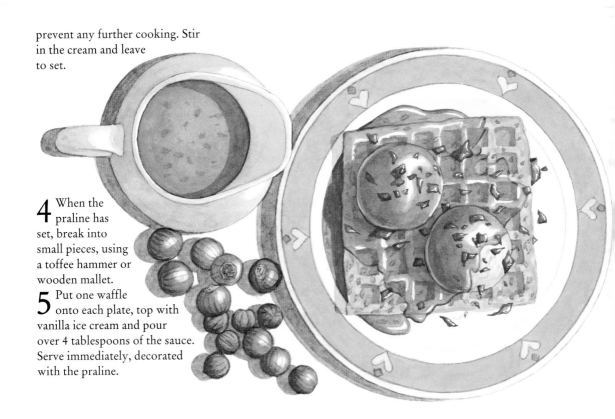

4 When the
praline has
set, break into
small pieces, using
a toffee hammer or
wooden mallet.

5 Put one waffle
onto each plate, top with
vanilla ice cream and pour
over 4 tablespoons of the sauce.
Serve immediately, decorated
with the praline.

EXOTIC FRUIT WAFFLES WITH CARDAMOM CREAM

This is for adults only! The sophisticated, fragrant combination of flavors will stun your guests. Passion fruit purée can be substituted for the fresh passion fruit. Any mix of exotic fruits can be used in the topping.

SERVES 6

15 passion fruit

½ quantity Traditional Waffle Batter (see page 26)

2 tbsp butter, melted

½ cup sugar

⅔ cup water

1 mango

10 lychees, canned or fresh, peeled and pitted

1 starfruit, cut into 12 slices

seeds from 9 crushed cardamom pods

1¼ cups whipping cream

1 Halve 12 of the passion fruit and press the flesh through a strainer into a bowl. Stir the purée into the batter.

2 Heat the waffle iron to medium and brush with some of the melted butter. Pour on enough batter to cover two-thirds of the iron and close the 2 halves. Cook for about 3 minutes, or 1½ minutes on each side if the iron is a manual one. Turn out onto a wire rack and keep warm in a low oven. Repeat to make 6 waffles.

3 Put the sugar and water into a pan and bring to a gentle boil, stirring frequently, to make a syrup. Cut the remaining passion fruit in half and press the flesh through a strainer into the syrup. Peel the mango and cut the flesh from the pit in chunks. Add to the syrup. Add the lychees and starfruit, and simmer for 5 minutes.

4 Remove the fruit with a slotted spoon and set aside. Boil the remaining syrup for 5 minutes until it thickens slightly.

5 Put the cardamom seeds into a bowl with the whipping cream. Whip until the cream just holds its own shape.

6 To serve, put a waffle on each serving plate, spoon over some fruit and syrup and spoon on whipped cream.

CHERRIES JUBILEE STACK

The grand finale! This is the greatest waffle of them all, and will bring gasps of delight at the table, where I defy any one person to finish a whole stack. This is a wonderful treat to give to children on the last day of the vacation.

SERVES 4

1 quantity Traditional Waffle Batter (see page 26)

1½ lb fresh cherries, pitted and rinsed, or
2 x 14 oz cans of pitted cherries in heavy syrup, drained and syrup reserved

½ cup granulated sugar

⅔ cup water

2 cups vanilla ice cream

1 Make 12 waffles from the batter. Turn out onto a wire rack and keep warm in a low oven.

2 If using fresh cherries, put the sugar and water into a pan and bring to the boil. When the sugar has dissolved, add the cherries and simmer until soft, about 10 minutes. Remove the cherries with a slotted spoon and reserve. Return the syrup to the boil and simmer for 8–10 minutes, until slightly thickened.

3 If using canned cherries, put ⅔ cup of the reserved syrup and the sugar into a pan, bring to the boil, and simmer for 12–15 minutes, then add the cherries to the pan.

4 Put a waffle on each serving plate and a scoop of vanilla ice cream, followed by another waffle and scoop of vanilla ice cream, and topped by a third waffle and scoop of ice cream. Spoon over a quarter of the

cherries and sauce. Serve
immediately.

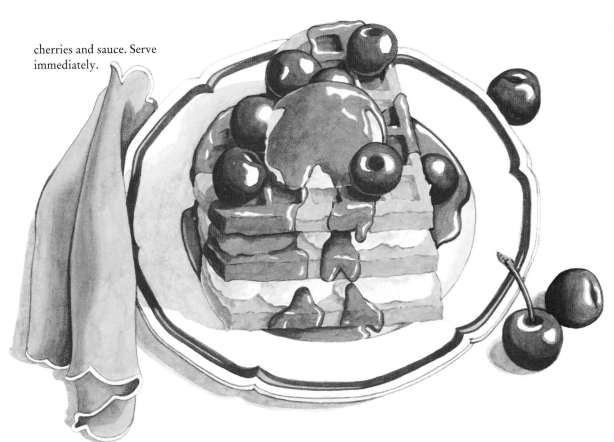

INDEX